CHECKERBOARD BIOGRAPHIES

JOANNA GAINES

PAIGE V. POLINSKY

Checkerboard Library

An Imprint of Abdo Publishing
abdobooks.com

ABDOBOOKS.COM

Published by Abdo Publishing, a division of ABDO, PO Box 398166, Minneapolis, Minnesota 55439.
Copyright © 2020 by Abdo Consulting Group, Inc. International copyrights reserved in all countries.
No part of this book may be reproduced in any form without written permission from the publisher.
Checkerboard Library™ is a trademark and logo of Abdo Publishing.

Printed in the United States of America, North Mankato, Minnesota
052019
092019

THIS BOOK CONTAINS
RECYCLED MATERIALS

Design and Production: Mighty Media, Inc.
Editor: Megan Borgert-Spaniol
Cover Photograph: Shutterstock Images
Interior Photographs: Alamy, p. 9; AP Images, pp. 5, 23, 25, 27, 28 (bottom left), 29 (top right); daveynin/
Flickr, p. 19; Everett Collection, pp. 15, 28 (top), 29 (bottom); Magnolia, pp. 7, 11, 28 (bottom right);
QuesterMark/Flickr, p. 13; Shutterstock Images, pp. 17, 21, 29 (top left)

Library of Congress Control Number: 2019934069

Publisher's Cataloging-in-Publication Data
Names: Polinsky, Paige V., author.
Title: Joanna Gaines / by Paige V. Polinsky
Description: Minneapolis, Minnesota : Abdo Publishing, 2020 | Series: Checkerboard biographies |
    Includes online resources and index.
Identifiers: ISBN 9781532119934 (lib. bdg.) | ISBN 9781532174797 (ebook)
Subjects: LCSH: Gaines, Joanna, 1978---Juvenile literature. | Television personalities--Biography--Juvenile
    literature. | Interior decorators--Biography--Juvenile literature. | Home repair and improvement--
    Juvenile literature. | Women entrepreneurs--Biography--Juvenile literature.
Classification: DDC 791.45092 [B]--dc23

CONTENTS

CHAPTER 1

HOME DESIGN STAR

Joanna Gaines is an interior designer, entrepreneur, and mother of five. She is best known for starring in the home-**renovation** TV show *Fixer Upper* with her husband, Chip. Chip led construction, and Gaines handled interior design.

Since the show first aired in 2014, Gaines' work has become a worldwide hit. Fans love her clean, simple designs. Though *Fixer Upper* ended in 2018, Gaines has never been busier. She and Chip run their family farm along with construction and **real estate** businesses.

Meanwhile, Gaines continues inspiring others to create spaces they love. Her home lifestyle empire includes lines of furniture, rugs, wallpaper, and more. Her Texas shopping **complex**, Magnolia Market at the **Silos**, sees more than 1.8 million visitors each year.

Joanna Gaines is always hard at work, searching for beauty in unexpected places. She is a design icon!

" I love to pull inspiration from what's around me. "

Gaines' "farmhouse chic" style mixes antiques with fresh, modern looks.

CHAPTER 2

TIRES & TV

Joanna Lea Stevens was born in Wichita, Kansas, on April 19, 1978. Her father, Jerry, is a US army **veteran**. He met Joanna's mother, Nan, while he was stationed in Korea. Joanna has two sisters, Teresa and Mary Kay.

Jerry worked for the tire company Firestone. His job brought the Stevens family to Waco, Texas, when Joanna was in high school. There, Jerry opened his own Firestone shop.

During high school, Joanna helped out at her father's shop. After graduating in 1997, she attended local McLennan Community College. While studying business, Joanna continued working with her father. She even starred in a few commercials for his tire shop. Many people have trouble speaking on camera, but Joanna was a natural. Filming the commercials sparked her interest in broadcasting.

KOREAN HERITAGE

Joanna's mom is Korean. When Joanna was a kid, classmates would tease her for being half-Korean. But by the time Joanna was in high school, she learned to be proud of her **heritage**.

BIO BASICS

NAME: Joanna Lea Gaines

NICKNAMES: Jo; Jojo

BIRTH: April 19, 1978, Wichita, Kansas

SPOUSE: Chip Gaines (2003-present)

CHILDREN: Drake, Ella Rose, Duke, Emmie Kay, and Crew

FAMOUS FOR: her role as co-star of the home-**renovation** TV show *Fixer Upper*; her interior design books, product lines, and shopping **complex**

ACHIEVEMENTS: nominated by the E! People's Choice Awards for favorite reality TV star; nominated by the Critics' Choice Awards for best reality show host (with Chip); created the Magnolia Foundation charity organization

CHAPTER 3

NEW YORK & BACK

Joanna transferred to Waco's Baylor University in 1998. There, she studied broadcast **journalism**. Joanna worked hard to gain broadcasting experience. She delivered news on the university's radio. She wrote and edited news stories while **interning** at a Waco TV station. She also worked on local radio and TV commercials.

In 2000, Joanna moved to New York City, New York, to intern for the hit news program *48 Hours*. Joanna worked long hours developing stories, and she often felt homesick. But exploring the big city's cozy home decor shops always lifted her spirits. She dreamed of opening her own **boutique** someday.

After graduating from Baylor in 2001, Joanna returned to the tire shop. She considered moving to a bigger city, but she loved Waco. She was not sure what she wanted to do next. Then she met Chip Gaines.

AS SEEN ON TV

Joanna dreamed of being on TV from an early age. As a kid, she would read the backs of cereal boxes out loud, pretending she was in commercials!

Gaines returned to New York City with Chip for their honeymoon. Years later, the couple visited the city to appear on NBC's *Today* show.

CHAPTER 4

DETERMINED DUO

Chip Gaines was a customer at Joanna's father's tire shop. He ran a laundry service and a **landscaping** business. He also **flipped** houses, which he then rented to college students. Chip was adventurous and took risks, while Joanna was quiet and careful. Although they were different, they got along well.

On May 31, 2003, Joanna married Chip and changed her name to Joanna Gaines. After their wedding, the couple moved into one of Chip's rental houses and remodeled it together. It was the first of many homes they would fix up as a team!

Gaines had no formal design training. Instead, she developed her sense of design through practice and experience. Gaines helped Chip style and decorate homes for his construction and **renovation**

THE LOOK

Many of Gaines' designs feature simple white walls and furniture. Gaines often uses barn doors and wooden boards to create a cozy farmhouse feeling. Chalkboards, houseplants, and plenty of light make her spaces complete!

Gaines has said that working with a spouse comes with challenges. But she feels she and Chip are a good team because they balance each other out.

business, Magnolia Homes. When she told him about her **boutique** idea, he encouraged her to go for it.

Gaines opened Magnolia Market in Waco in 2003. The little shop sold housewares and home decor. Shoppers loved Gaines' clean, simple style. Magnolia Market was a hit!

In 2005, Gaines and Chip had their first child, Drake. Gaines became a mom on the move. In addition to running Magnolia Market, she hunted for new items to sell at the store. Gaines often searched **thrift stores** for affordable treasures. Sometimes she restored old pieces of furniture herself.

Business was booming. But in 2006, Gaines decided to close Magnolia Market. She was expecting another child and wanted to focus on her family. Soon after closing the shop, she had a daughter, Ella Rose.

The next year, a **recession** hit the United States. Many people could not afford new homes, and the Gaineses had trouble selling **flips**. So, they focused on remodeling projects instead. Gaines and Chip helped customers make old homes feel new. The Magnolia Homes goal was "to make Waco beautiful one house at a time!"

Gaines and Chip had another son, Duke, in 2008. As their family grew, so did their businesses. Over the

 We think home is kind of a big deal. If we can inspire people in their own homes, that's huge for us. "

In early 2019, Gaines took on the restoration of a historic treasure. She and Chip purchased a castle in Waco that was built in 1890!

next year, they started a **real estate** company, Magnolia Realty. They also welcomed another daughter, Emmie Kay, in 2010.

CHAPTER 5

FIXER UPPER

The Gaineses kept busy working on flips. In 2012, a friend sent photos of their current project to a popular blog. TV producer Katie Neff saw the post and contacted Gaines. Neff wanted to film the Gaineses for a home improvement TV show.

A couple weeks later, Neff's crew arrived to film a flip. The first few days were bumpy. Chip was shy on camera, so Gaines had to take the lead. But popular TV channel HGTV saw **potential** in the Gaineses.

Gaines and Chip filmed an **episode**, transforming an old building into a beautiful home. When the episode aired in May 2013, more than 1.9 million viewers tuned in! The Gaineses filmed 12 more episodes over the next year.

Season one of *Fixer Upper* aired in April 2014. While Gaines and Chip remodeled Waco homes, they also **renovated** an

WACO OR BUST

HGTV wanted to film *Fixer Upper* in bigger Texas cities, such as Austin and Dallas. But Gaines and Chip refused to travel far from their family and businesses. They convinced HGTV to base the show in Waco instead.

While the Gaineses kept their businesses local, they traveled out of state to give TV interviews.

old farmhouse for themselves. Settling on a farm was a longtime dream for the couple.

Viewers loved watching Gaines and Chip at work. Each week, millions of people tuned in to see their teamwork and warm personalities.

CHAPTER 6

WACO WONDERS

Despite her busy life, Gaines missed running **Magnolia Market.** So in May 2014, she reopened the shop. *Fixer Upper* fans were soon swarming the market. Gaines also launched an online store for faraway customers. But she soon had an even bigger vision.

That fall, Gaines noticed two rusty **silos** and some old, empty buildings across from her children's school. Right away, she had a plan. She and Chip could move all of their Magnolia businesses to those buildings!

The buildings were not for sale, but Gaines was determined. She explained her idea to the owner. When she promised not to tear the buildings down, the owner agreed to sell.

Gaines and Chip bought the property in November 2014. It was a big, risky project. But they believed they could create something special.

HOMETOWN HEROES

In November 2014, Waco mayor Malcolm Duncan Jr. presented Gaines and Chip with a key to the city. The key was a token of gratitude for the Gaines' positive promotion of Waco.

The new Magnolia Market property included a big green lawn. The lawn served as a central space for visitors to relax and play games.

Season two of *Fixer Upper* aired in January 2015. By then, tourists were visiting Waco from all over the country. Meanwhile, the Gaineses were busy **renovating** their new property. It would be the future home of Magnolia Market!

In October 2015, Gaines and Chip opened Magnolia Market at the **Silos**. The downtown shopping **complex** was unlike anything Waco had ever seen. A giant barn featured Gaines' new shop with room to spare. Gaines used the extra space to host monthly markets featuring local sellers.

The property's grounds included a food truck park, a full garden, and a stage for events. Gaines wanted the Silos to be more than a place to shop. Her goal was to help visitors create happy memories with their loved ones. "Hopefully people leave inspired to dream big," she said.

Gaines and Chip were shining a light on the city of Waco. In December 2015, the magazine *Waco Today* named them "Persons of the Year." The third

AN EVENING WITH GAINES

In October 2014, Gaines hosted Magnolia Market's first workshop. She served food to her guests and showed them table-setting ideas. Of the 600 attendees, nearly half came from out of state!

By 2017, Magnolia Market at the Silos attracted an average of 30,000 visitors a week.

season of *Fixer Upper* aired that same month, and Gaines' designs impressed viewers more than ever. *Fixer Upper* became the highest-rated show on HGTV!

CHAPTER 7

BEYOND HGTV

By 2016, homeowners everywhere were asking the Gaineses for help. Gaines and Chip were too busy to travel. They wanted to stay in Waco with their children. But Gaines found a different way to help.

In January, Gaines launched a line of furniture and home decor called Magnolia Home. *Fixer Upper* fans could now create her "farmhouse **chic**" look on their own! Gaines said of the line, "This is our way of coming to your town without really having to come to your town."

Interior design was just one of Gaines' talents. She wanted to share other ways to create a sense of home. In July 2016, Gaines opened **Silos** Baking Co. The bakery offered sweet treats made with her favorite family recipes.

Gaines also continued exploring other types of design.

MAGNOLIA HOUSE

In February 2016, Gaines and Chip began taking reservations for Magnolia House. The bed-and-breakfast was a **renovation** project just outside Waco. Within a few hours, it was booked solid for the next six months!

In 2017, Gaines and Chip announced a new partnership with retail giant Target. Soon after, Target stores launched the home decor collection Hearth & Hand with Magnolia.

In December 2016, she released a line of children's dresses through the company Matilda Jane Clothing. The colorful clothes were inspired by her daughters and their life on the family farm.

CHAPTER 8

BEHIND THE DESIGN

While the Gaineses pursued their many projects, their show received critical **acclaim**. In July 2017, *Fixer Upper* received an Emmy nomination for "Outstanding Structured Reality Program." Though the show was popular, big changes were ahead.

That September, Gaines and Chip announced *Fixer Upper* would end after season five. Fans were heartbroken. Many worried that the Gaineses were divorcing. But the couple denied these rumors.

While filming *Fixer Upper*'s final season, Gaines created another series. *Fixer Upper: Behind the Design* gave viewers a peek behind the scenes of *Fixer Upper*. It captured Gaines' design process for the season five projects. The series included rooms not featured in the original show. It also showed Gaines working closely with her design team.

CHILDREN AT PLAY

Raising children changed Gaines' style. She loved clean, white spaces but realized they did not suit her lifestyle. Gaines began designing more colorful, creative spaces her whole family could enjoy.

In October 2016, Gaines and Chip published *The Magnolia Story*. The book is about their journey as life and business partners.

Through it all, family remained Gaines' number-one focus. On Instagram, she often shared moments from home. Fans loved seeing Gaines and her children cook, pick flowers, and care for their farm animals. In fact, Gaines was ranked the most popular TV personality on social media several times in 2017!

CHAPTER 9

HARDWORKING HOMEBODY

Gaines and Chip kept chasing big dreams together. After a popular Waco restaurant closed in 2016, they had bought the building and began **renovations**. In February 2018, they reopened it as Magnolia Table. This restaurant featured fresh, local food. Some of the produce and eggs came right from Gaines' home garden! Before long, Gaines published a cookbook called *Magnolia Table*.

Fixer Upper officially came to an end in April 2018. The Gaineses were sad to say goodbye, but they were also ready for a new beginning. That June, the family welcomed their fifth child, Crew.

As a mom of five, Gaines was busier than ever. But she called

MAGNOLIA WAREHOUSE

In March 2018, Gaines reopened her original Magnolia Market location as the Magnolia Warehouse Shop. It sold discontinued or slightly damaged home goods at low prices.

Magnolia Table took over the space of the Elite Cafe, a diner that had served Waco patrons since 1941.

Crew her "second wind." In November 2018, Gaines published an interior design guide called *Homebody*. The book encourages readers to discover their own personal design styles.

CHAPTER 10

NO PLACE LIKE HOME

Despite the end of *Fixer Upper*, the Gaines family would not be gone from TV for long. In November 2018, Gaines and Chip announced their next big project. The couple was creating their own home lifestyle network. Much of the filming would be in Waco, and their children would play a big role.

While Gaines manages a busy career, she works hard to spend time with her kids. The family cooks, gardens, and even writes together. In March 2019, Gaines and her kids released a children's book. *We Are the Gardeners* is based on their adventures growing a garden together.

Despite their popularity, Gaines and Chip do not see themselves as a "celebrity family." They want their children to understand the importance of hard work and helping others. And for Gaines, this starts at home.

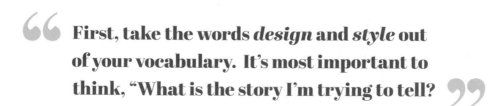

First, take the words *design* and *style* out of your vocabulary. It's most important to think, "What is the story I'm trying to tell?

Gaines and Chip have a charity called the Magnolia Foundation. It works to improve the lives of children, families, and communities through restoration.

TIMELINE

1978

Joanna Lea Stevens is born in Wichita, Kansas, on April 19.

2001

Joanna graduates from Baylor University in Texas.

2003

Joanna marries Chip Gaines and changes her last name to Gaines. She opens Magnolia Market.

2013

Gaines and Chip film the first season of *Fixer Upper*.

2014

Season one of *Fixer Upper* airs. Gaines reopens Magnolia Market and launches an online store.

2017

Gaines begins filming her new show *Fixer Upper: Behind the Design.*

2015

Gaines and Chip open Magnolia Market at the Silos.

2019

Gaines releases a children's book called *We Are the Gardeners.*

2016

Gaines launches Magnolia Home and opens Silos Baking Co.

2018

Gaines opens Magnolia Table. *Fixer Upper* ends and Gaines publishes *Homebody.*

GLOSSARY

acclaim—approval or praise.

boutique—a small, fashionable store.

chic—fashionable or stylish.

complex—a building or a group of buildings with related units.

entrepreneur—one who organizes, manages, and accepts the risks of a business or an enterprise.

episode—one show in a television series.

flip—to buy, renovate, and resell at a higher price. A house that has been flipped is sometimes called a flip.

heritage—something handed down from one generation to the next.

intern—to gain guided practical experience in a professional field.

journalism—the collecting and editing of news to be presented through various media. These include newspapers, magazines, television, and radio.

landscaping—the improving of the natural beauty of an area of land.

potential—a quality that someone or something has that can be developed or used.

real estate—property, including buildings and land.

recession—a period of time when business activity slows.

renovate—to restore by rebuilding or repairing.

silo—a tall, round tower used to store items.

thrift store—a store that sells used items.

veteran—a person who has served in the armed forces.

ONLINE RESOURCES

Booklinks
NONFICTION NETWORK
FREE! ONLINE NONFICTION RESOURCES

To learn more about Joanna Gaines, please visit **abdobooklinks.com** or scan this QR code. These links are routinely monitored and updated to provide the most current information available.

INDEX